FOLENS FLYING STAR
Starting Key Stage 2 English

CONTENTS

2	Handwriting 1	14	Blends
3	Playful pairs	15	The case of the missing letters
4	The Brave Little Tailor (story)	16	Passport
5	The Brave Little Tailor (questions)	17	Spell 'ea' words
6	Handwriting 2	18	Action words
7	Feeling sheepish	19	Handwriting 4
8	'ed' and 'ing'	20	Number plates
9	Mischief zoo	21	Asking questions
10	Handwriting 3	22	Handwriting 5
11	Crossword puzzle	23	Wordsearch
12	The Lion and the Mouse (story)	24	Antonyms – opposites
13	The Lion and the Mouse (questions)	25	On holiday
		26	The swallows
		27	When?
		28	How do you get there?

Folens books are protected by international copyright laws. All rights are reserved. The copyright of all materials in this book, except where otherwise stated, remains the property of the publisher and authors.
No part of this publication may be reproduced, stored in a retrieval system, or transmitted, in any form or by any means, for whatever purpose, without the written permission of Folens Limited.
© 1994 Folens Limited, on behalf of the authors.
First published 1994 by Folens Limited, Dunstable and Dublin.
ISBN 1 85276719-7
Folens Limited, Apex Business Centre, Boscombe Road, Dunstable, LU5 4RL, England.

© Folens.

Handwriting 1

fit lit light

AlexRussell

fish   fish

AL
Alex

Playful pairs

Vowels like to go about in pairs.
Sometimes two of the same go together!
Can you finish off these words?
Some have 'oo' in the middle,
Some have 'ee'.

'ee'
1. feet
2. sweet
3. creep
4. deep
5. bee
6. peel
7. seeds
8. bleed
9. been
10. sleep
11. green
12. need
13. week
14. peep
15. seem
16. sheep

'oo'
1. door
2. food
3. good
4. boot
5. look
6. pool
7. fool
8. roof
9. moon
10. shoots
11. roots
12. room
13. cool
14. soon

How well did I do?

© Folens.

The Brave Little Tailor

• Read the story and answer the questions on page 5.

One morning, a tailor was sitting at his window working, when an old woman came down the road. She was crying, "Honey for sale! Honey for sale!"
It was nearly lunch time.
The tailor thought honey would be nice on his bread. So he put his head out of the window and called, "Here, my good woman. I'll have some honey."
The old woman hurried over to the tailor, and he bought some honey.
He put the honey on a slice of bread, put the bread on the table near him, and carried on with his work.

Brave   Tailor   bread

How well did I do?

The Brave Little Tailor

- Answer these questions about the story on page 4.

1. What work was the tailor doing? _____
   _____
   _____

2. Who came down the road? _____
   _____

3. What was the old woman selling? _____
   _____

4. What time of the day was it? _____
   _____

5. Did the tailor like honey? _____

6. What did the tailor do with the honey? _____
   _____
   _____

7. Where did he put the slice of bread? _____
   _____

- Write the missing letters **br**.

_ _ ush

_ _ oom

_ _ ead

_ _ other

How well did I do?

Handwriting 2

Practise these.

How well did I do?

Feeling sheepish

Look at the speech bubbles.

- Look at the picture sequence and read the text.
- Write in the text the words that are spoken.

Farmer Trotter was surprised when he entered the kitchen. He shouted, "___ ___ ___ ___ ___ ___?"

Farmer Trotter was angry. He called, "___ ___ ___ ___ ___ ___ ___?"

He wad hopping mad when the sheep answered, "___ ___ ___ ___ ___ ___."

When Farmer Trotter found Boy Blue, he roared, "___ ___ ___ ___ ___ ___. ___ ___ ___ ___."

How well did I do?

'ed' and 'ing'

We can add '**ed**' and '**ing**' to verbs to make new words.

I jump.

I am jump**ing**.

I jump**ed**.

- Complete the boxes by following the rules.

1. For some words, just add '**ed**' and '**ing**' to make new words.

play	played	playing
crack		
look		
fish		
kick		
cook		
mend		

2. After a single vowel and a single consonant, double the last letter and add **ed** and **ing**.

shop	shopped	shopping
trip		
hop		
clap		
chop		
chat		
rub		

3. When a word ends in magic '**e**', drop the '**e**' and add '**ed**' and '**ing**'.

like	liked	liking
hope		
love		
save		
blame		
dine		
smile		

How well did I do?

Mischief zoo

ferocious **wriggly** **striped**
naughty **flying** **talking**

Do not walk across the _____ zebra.

Do not teach the _____ parrots rude words.

_____ snakes should not be used as scarves.

The _____ bats should not be used for cricket.

This cage is reserved for _____ children.

Heads put in the _____ lion's mouth cannot be replaced.

The monkeys have stolen the adjectives from the signs.

- Help the zookeeper by putting each adjective in the right place.

How well did I do?

Handwriting 3

a b c d e (f) g
h i j (k) l m n
o p q r s t u v
w x (y) z

Here is the alphabet.

Look at the letters f, k and y.

Practise f, k and y.

f f f f f f f

k k k k k k k

y y y y y y y

How well did I do?

Crossword puzzle

- Read the clues and write in the answers.

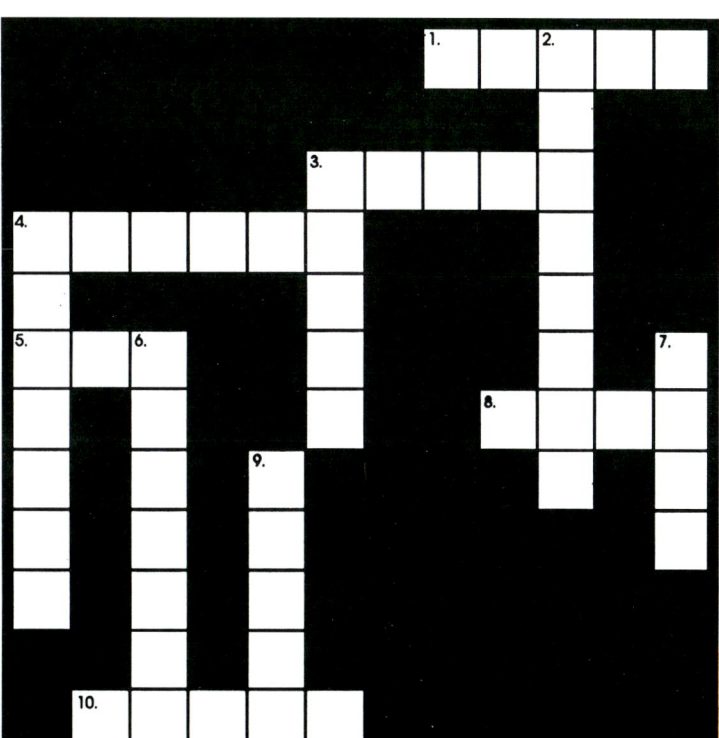

Across

1. You can push somebody on this. (5)
3. You can dig the sand with this. (5)
4. You go here to learn. (6)
5. You kick the ball into this. (3)
8. You can throw and catch this. (4)
10. It is green. You can play ball on it. (5)

Down

2. You eat this from a cone. (3, 5)
3. The children play on this. (5)
4. You can make sand castles in this. (4, 3)
6. She helps you learn. (7)
7. The sky is this colour. (4)
9. They have leaves and branches. (5)

How well did I do?

The Lion and the Mouse

- Read the story and answer the questions on page 13.

One day a lion was asleep under a tree. A little mouse ran over his paw. The lion lifted his paw to crush the mouse.
"Please, please, do not kill me," squeaked the mouse.
The lion took pity on her.
"Thank you," said the mouse, "one day I will help you."
"Ha, ha, ha," laughed the lion. "A little mouse like you, help the king of the jungle."
Some days later, the lion walked into a trap. He could not free himself. He roared and roared. Suddenly, he heard a little squeak. The mouse was beside him. She nibbled at the ropes and in no time the lion was free.
The lion thanked the mouse.
"You have saved my life," he said.
The lion and the mouse became great friends.

squeak
suddenly
roared
please
laughed

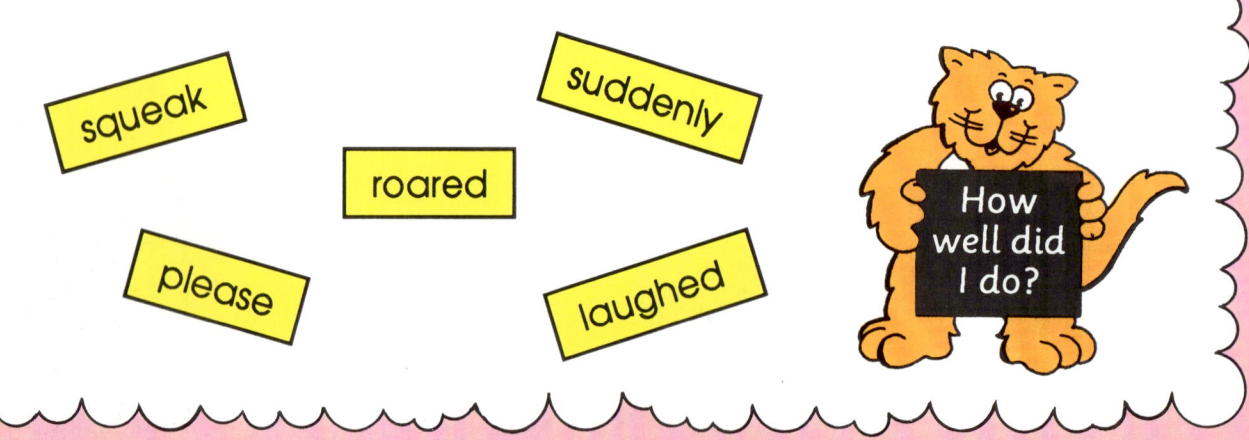

How well did I do?

The Lion and the Mouse

- Answer these questions about the story on page 12.

1. Where was the lion asleep? _____

2. What ran over the lion's paw? _____
   _____

3. What was the lion going to do? _____
   _____

4. What did the mouse say to the lion? _____
   _____

5. Did the lion believe the mouse? _____

6. What happened to the lion some days later? _____
   _____

7. What did the lion do when he could not free himself? _____
   _____

8. How did the mouse free the lion? _____
   _____

9. What did the lion say to the mouse? _____
   _____

10. Did the lion and the mouse become friends? _____
    _____

How well did I do?

Blends

Sometimes 3 consonants go together.
You can still hear the 3 sounds.

spl **scr** **spr** **str**

1. Here are some useful words beginning with these blends. Read them. Sort the words, and write them in the correct boxes below.

spring   scrub   sprout   splash   strong

stream   strap   spread   splendid   scrape

scrap   screw   string   splinter   spray

spl	scr	spr	str

2. Find the correct word for the pictures.

spl _____

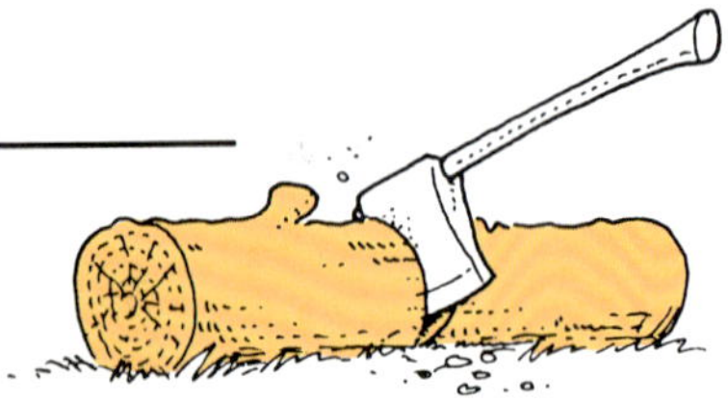

spr _____

str _____

scr _____

How well did I do?

14

The case of the missing letters

Letters have been missed out of these words.

- Help Sherlock by marking with an apostrophe where the letter is missing.
- Write the matching words.

  The first one is done for you.

  don't $\longrightarrow$ do not

  doesnt $\longrightarrow$ _____

  Ill $\longrightarrow$ _____

  whats $\longrightarrow$ _____

  Im $\longrightarrow$ _____

  shes $\longrightarrow$ _____

  cant $\longrightarrow$ _____

- Think of some more.

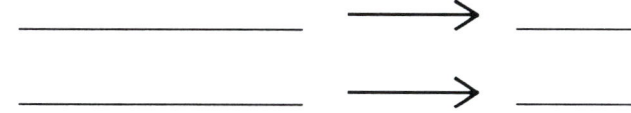

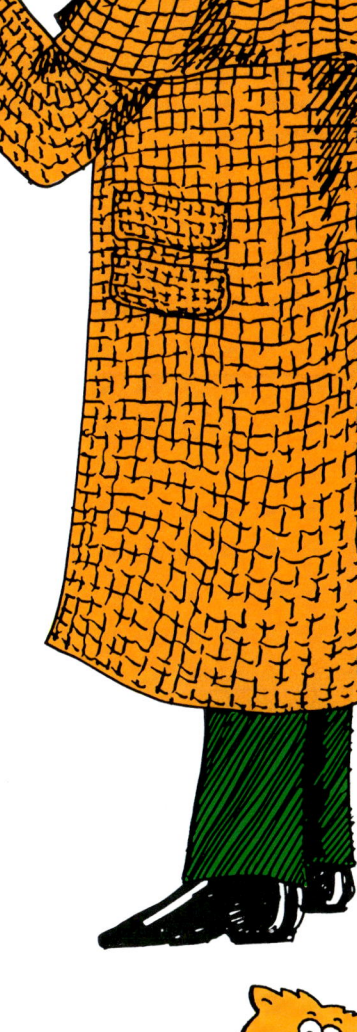

  _____ $\longrightarrow$ _____

  _____ $\longrightarrow$ _____

  _____ $\longrightarrow$ _____

How well did I do?

Passport

Photo of bearer

Passport number ME008

Signature _____

Bearer

Name _____
Address _____
_____
Nationality _____
Place of birth _____
Date of birth _____
Height _____
Weight _____
Hair colour _____
Eye colour _____
Special marks _____

Spell 'ea' words

Sometimes '**ea**' sounds like '**ee**'.
Here are some useful '**ea**' words.

1. Read the words. Spell the words without looking.

   leaves   team   please

   _____   _____   _____

   read   steam   sea

   _____   _____   _____

   tea   east   seat

   _____   _____   _____

2. Put 3 '**ea**' words together in one sentence.

   _____

heat	meat	eat
beach	each	peach
steal	meal	real
team	dream	ice-cream

3. Here are some '**ea**' words.
   Read the words. Spell the words without looking.

   lead   clean   beam   deal

   _____   _____   _____   _____

   reach   stream   squeal   teacher

   _____   _____   _____   _____

   speak   cheap   easy   mean

   _____   _____   _____   _____

How well did I do?

© Folens.

Action!

Action words

Action words are words which tell us about the actions of a person, place, animal or thing. **Action** words are 'doing' words.

Examples: The boy **ran**.
The town **was** empty.
The dog **barks**.
The ball **is rolling**.

A • Underline the **action** words in these sentences.

1. The cat chased the mouse.
2. The farmer bought a new horse.
3. The bus is coming down the road.
4. We went to London Zoo.
5. The light was shining in the dark.
6. Her brother fell and broke his arm.
7. The cow jumped over the moon.
8. A small bird sang in the tree.

B • Write an **action** word to fill the blank spaces.

1. The baby _____ all night
2. The police _____ the robber.
3. The lion _____ the deer.
4. A tree _____ in our garden.
5. Sean _____ a long letter.
6. The old man _____ the dog a bone.
7. His uncle _____ in Exeter.
8. The Irish team _____ the match.

How well did I do?

18   © Folens.

Handwriting 4

l l l l

lions

Some lions like to leap for fun in the sun.

Some extra practice.

l l

l

How well did I do?

Number plates

MAL 1 **FOL 20**

Sometimes you can make words up from car number plates, by adding other letters. **Keep the letters in the same order.**

s t u n n e d

s e a t e d

i n s i s t e d

s t r a i n e d

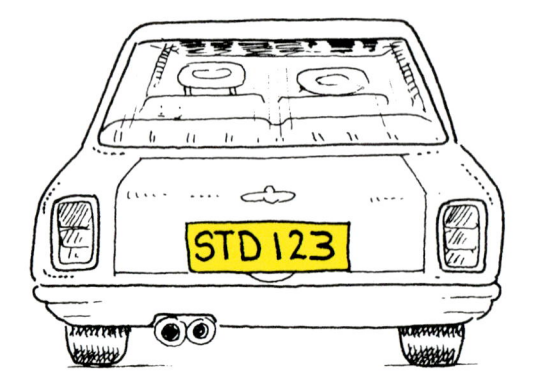

s t a n d

S a t u r d a y

s t a n d a r d

a s s i s t e d

(STD 123)

- See how many words you can make from these number plates.

Keep the letters in the same order.

ARK 46

SON 32

DNL 81

PTR 11

BTF 57

B RD 1

How well did I do?

Asking questions

- Did you see that foul
- Is it nearly half-time
- You'll never walk alone
- Come on reds, you can do it
- The goalie couldn't catch a cold
- Is the referee stupid
- Who wants a programme
- This is really exciting
- Where can I buy a pie
- Lift me up I can't see

- Decide which of these sentences are questions.
- Put a question mark at the end of each question.
- Put a full stop at the end of the others.

How well did I do?

Handwriting 5

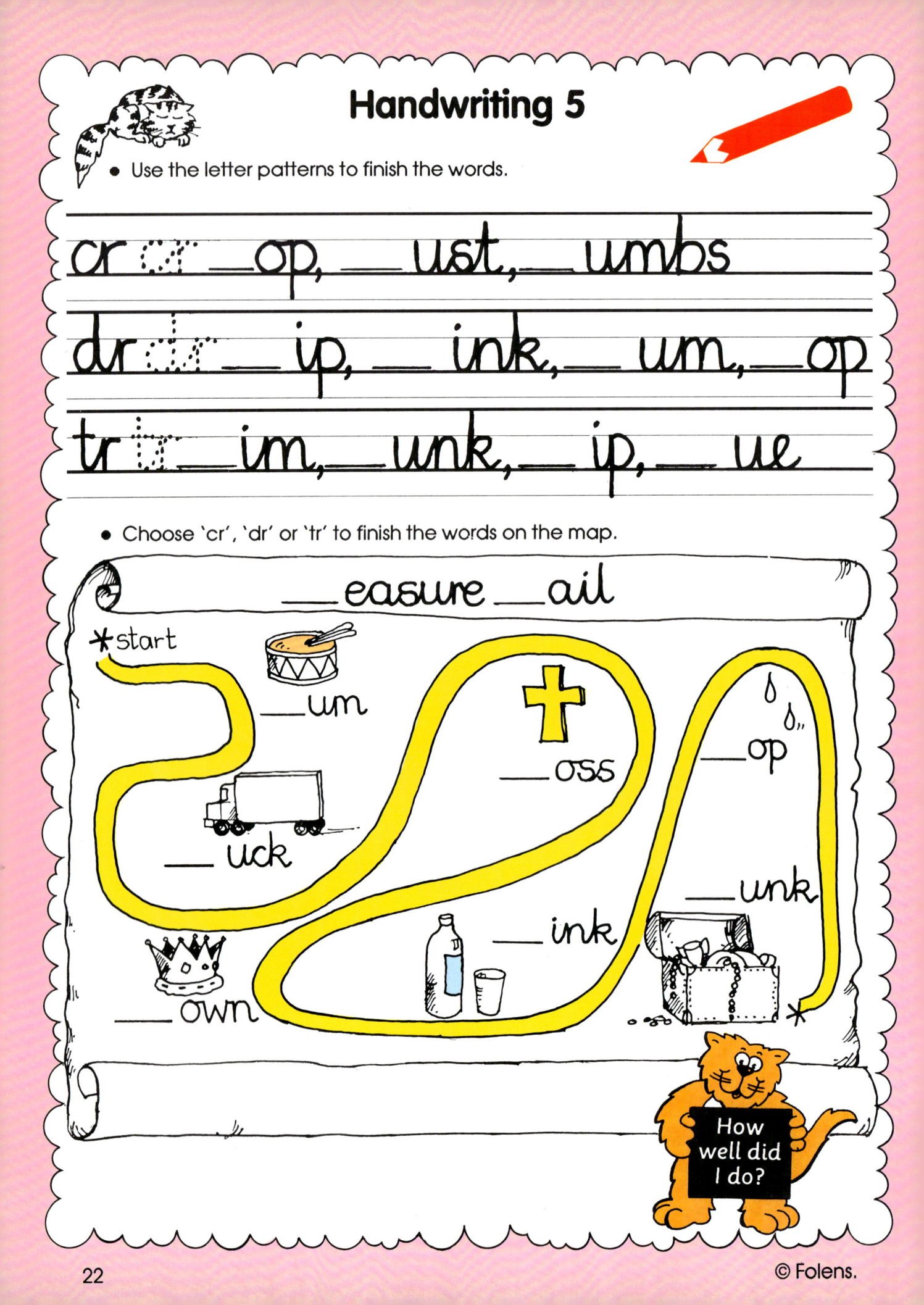

- Use the letter patterns to finish the words.

cr cr __op, __ust, __umbs

dr dr __ip, __ink, __um, __op

tr tr __im, __unk, __ip, __ue

- Choose 'cr', 'dr' or 'tr' to finish the words on the map.

__easure __ail

*start

__um

__oss

__op

__uck

__ink

__unk

__own

How well did I do?

22 © Folens.

Wordsearch

Learn to spell like this:

Look   Say   Cover   Write   Check

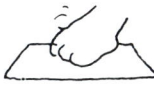

1. Here are some words to spell
   • Read the words. Spell the words.

went	have	said	was
after	with	little	very
are	give	come	want

2. Find the words in the wordsearch. All the words go across. →
   • Put a ring round the word when you find it.
   • Cross the words off as you go along.

went   with
        little
have   very
        after
was
        come
        said
are
        give
        want

a	c	a	r	e	o	w	i	t	h	e
r	p	w	w	e	n	t	i	n	c	e
c	g	i	v	e	w	w	a	n	t	i
w	l	i	t	l	e	a	f	t	e	r
g	h	a	v	e	a	w	a	h	t	n
m	t	o	n	w	l	i	t	t	l	e
s	h	s	a	i	d	w	g	i	v	w
a	w	e	c	o	m	e	g	n	a	r
a	w	v	e	r	y	o	w	a	s	r

3. Which 4 words begin with 'w'?

_____

Which 2 words have 3 letters?

_____

Which word has 5 letters?

_____

How well did I do?

© Folens.   23

Antonyms – opposites

Big is the opposite of **little**.

Big   little

1. Find all the words which are opposites. Write them in pairs on the lines. The first one is done for you. Cross off the words as you go along.

Learn to spell like this:

Look   Say    Cover    Write    Check

~~up~~   fast   light   right   over   new
top   low   left   under   before   cold
high   slow   thin   old   after   ~~down~~   dark
back   front   bottom   fat   hot

up _____   down _____   _____   _____

_____   _____   _____   _____

_____   _____   _____   _____

_____   _____   _____   _____

_____   _____   _____   _____

_____   _____   _____   _____

2. Choose 4 words. Put each word into a sentence.

1. _____
2. _____
3. _____
4. _____

Note: Synonyms are **words meaning the same thing**: big, huge, large, enormous. A thesaurus is a dictionary full of synonyms.

24   © Folens.

On holiday

- You are going on a seaside holiday to Tunisia. It will be hot and sunny every day.

- Pack only the items you will need.

- Complete the chart below.

Items to be taken	
Item	Reason

Items to be left	
Item	Reason

© Folens.

The swallows

- Read the passage and answer the questions.

Evening had come. The big, red sun was beginning to go down. A tired farmer was walking slowly across the fields. He stopped to look at the swallows. These tiny birds were still darting and diving through the air, hunting for food. But flies were getting scarce. Soon the swallows would leave on their long flight across the sea. Swallows leave us in the autumn, but many birds stay with us. These birds eat berries and seeds, so they can do without little flies. The blackbird likes to eat the rowan berries. A thrush prefers to eat ripe blackberries. The robin loves a feed of rosehips! At the back of the farmer's house there was an old barn. Last May, the swallows had made their nests there. It was now September and the barn was full of hay. But the nests were empty. The baby swallows had left their cosy homes. The farmer stood still as he watched these young swallows fly above him. With long, strong wings they moved through the sky like lightning. Tomorrow, they will be gone. But next spring they will return.

1. What do swallows eat? _____

2. How is it that some birds can do without flies? _____

3. On what does the blackbird feed? _____

4. Which bird likes rosehips? _____

5. Where was the old barn? _____

6. When did the swallows build their nests? _____

7. Why does the swallow have such long, strong wings? _____

8. When will the swallows return? _____

How well did I do?

When?

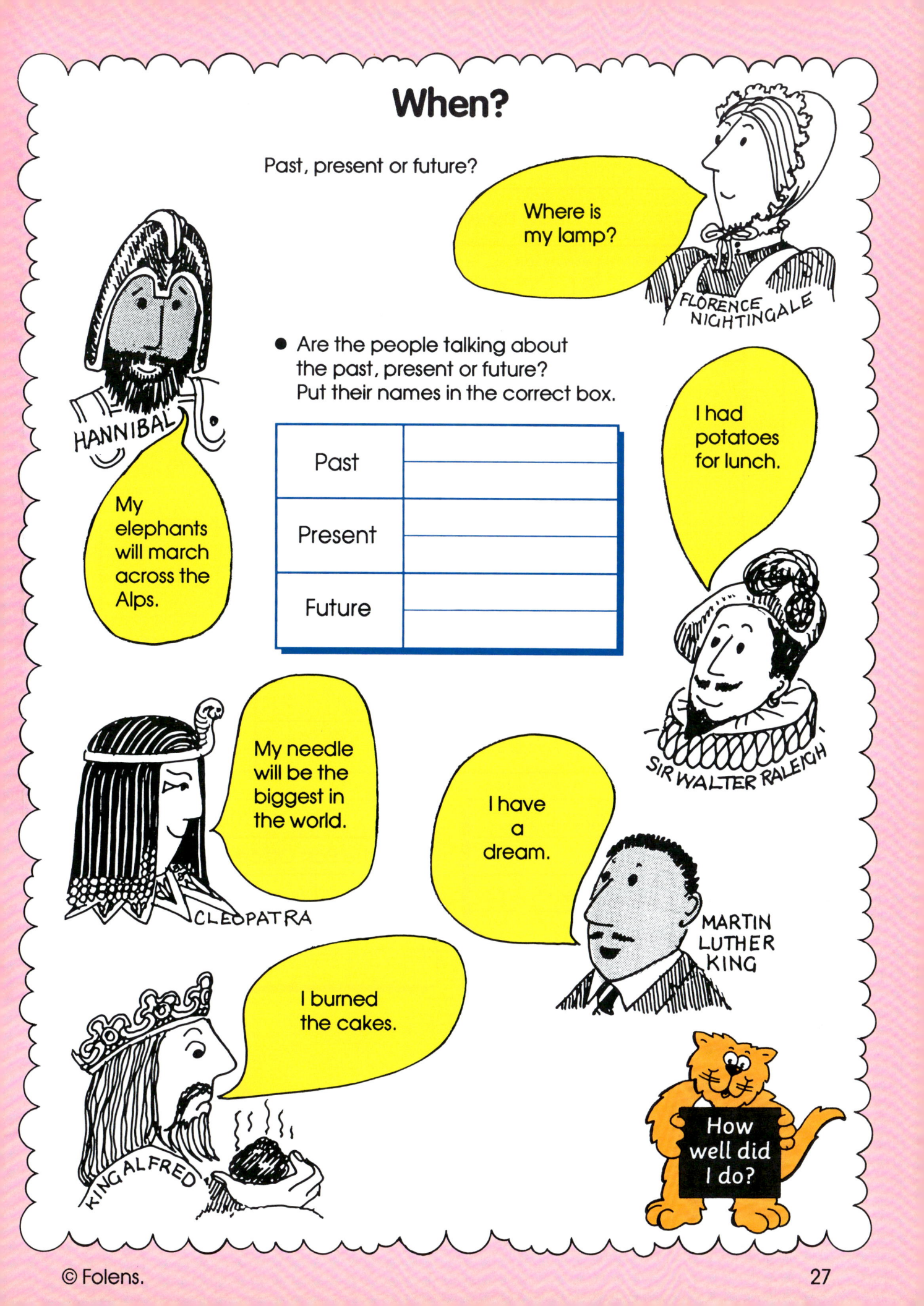

Past, present or future?

Florence Nightingale: Where is my lamp?

Hannibal: My elephants will march across the Alps.

- Are the people talking about the past, present or future? Put their names in the correct box.

Past	
Present	
Future	

Sir Walter Raleigh: I had potatoes for lunch.

Cleopatra: My needle will be the biggest in the world.

Martin Luther King: I have a dream.

King Alfred: I burned the cakes.

How well did I do?

How do you get there?

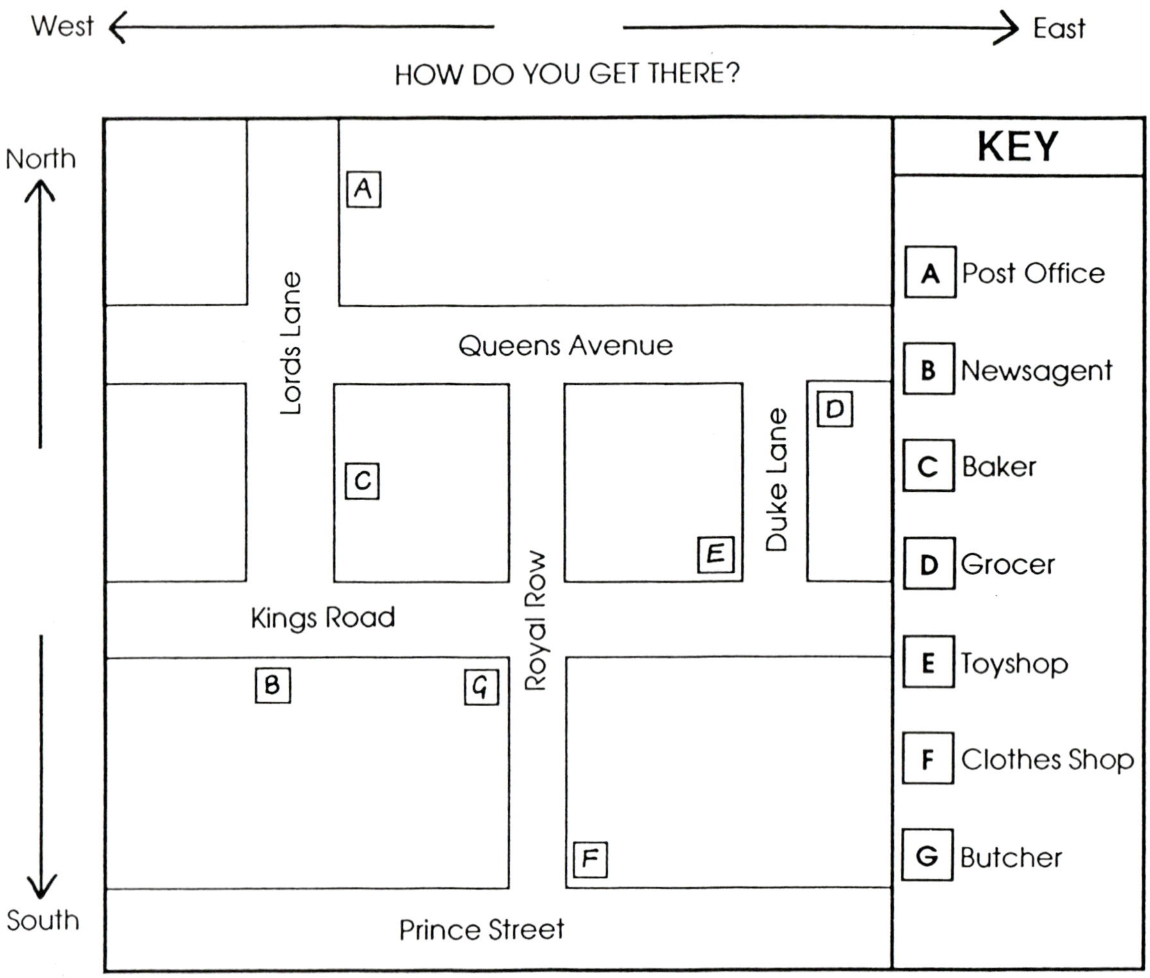
West
East
HOW DO YOU GET THERE?
North
South
Queens Avenue
Kings Road
Prince Street
Lords Lane
Royal Row
Duke Lane
A
B
C
D
E
F
G
KEY
A Post Office
B Newsagent
C Baker
D Grocer
E Toyshop
F Clothes Shop
G Butcher

Follow these instructions
Start at F
Walk **north** along Royal Row.
Turn **west** at Kings Road.
Walk along Kings Road.
Walk **north** up Lords Lane.
Turn **east** at Queens Avenue.
Walk along Queens Avenue.
Stop at the shop after Duke Lane.
Where are you?

Give instructions
from the Post Office
to the butcher's.

How well did I do?

Folens Flying Start
Starting Key Stage 2 English

Guidance for parents and carers

The children's pages provide activities which will help to develop skills in English: reading, writing for different purposes, including writing instructions and filling in forms, spelling, and handwriting. It is also important that children develop skills in speaking and listening, which of course, is difficult if they are only writing. You may like to use some of the ideas for discussion questioning, listening to and following instructions. The activities have been carefully selected to cover a large range of ability levels, and are arranged so that they become progressively more difficult towards the end of the book. Your child may find some of them very easy and some too difficult. Noticing his/her achievement will help you to decide which books would provide the support which s/he needs.

Workbooks are intended for children to write or draw in. The following notes provide suggestions as to how everyday situations may be used to develop children's language skills.

Reading together

- You may need to read or explain the instructions, especially if the child is just beginning to read, to ensure that s/he understands what to do. Look for the symbol.

Working together

- Whenever possible, work with your child. For some activities this is particularly important. Look for the symbol.

- Choose a time when the child (and you!) are relaxed, and not already engaged in any other activity.
- Work in a comfortable place.
- Attempt only one or two activities, unless the child wishes to continue. Children learn best when they are interested! Remember that the time for which chidren can concentrate varies. As a rule the younger the child, the shorter his/her concentration, but even the youngest children may surprise you if something really captures their interest. Watch for signs of restlessness, and stop!
- Read the parents'/carers' pages, and the children's pages, in preparation, before the child begins.
- Try, whenever appropriate, to relate the activities in the book to everyday life, sometimes before the child has attempted the activity, sometimes afterwards, but do not make the mistake of turning every occasion into a lesson! Some ideas are suggested below.
- Answers are provided here, but the value of any language activity does not just lie in 'getting the right answer'. Skills will be developed during the process of the activity, whether or not the correct answer is achieved. Discussion helps the learner to sort out his/her ideas.
- Praise the child for his/her achievement. Avoid becoming irritable/sounding disappointed if s/he finds an activity too difficult. You could say, "You'll be able to do that when you've had more practice." On completion of each page ask the child to choose a sticker to show how well s/he has done and to stick it in the box provided.

Handwriting 1 - (*page 2*)
Some practice for children who are using unjoined print. The child should trace the outlines of the letters and words shown in dotted lines, then copy them in the spaces provided. Ensure that the child is seated comfortably at a table or desk of the right height, and has space to move his/her writing hand easily across the page from left to right.

Playful pairs - (*page 3*) (Spelling)
Prepare for this by drawing attention to words with 'oo' and 'ee' sounds, spelt as shown. Names of things around the home, in the shops, park, street, etc, may be used: food, cheese, balloon, street, beef, sheet, roof, stool, settee, cooler, spoon. A useful follow up would be to list words with the same sounds but spelt differently e.g. meat, beans, gear, seat, soup. Children who find this activity difficult could begin with *Key Stage 1 Spelling*. *Key Stage 2 Spelling* begins at this level but soon progresses to more challenging activities.
Answers:
'**ee**'
feet, sweet, creep, deep, bee, peel, seeds, bleed, been, sleep, green, need, week, peep, seem, sheep.
'**oo**'
door, food, good, boot, look, pool, fool, roof, moon, shoots, roots, room, cool, soon.

© Folens.

The Brave Little Tailor - (*pages 4-5*) (Reading)
Here is the opening of a well known story. The entire story may be found in *Folens Busy Beaver Books: Stage 2, Book 5*. *Key Stage 2 Reading* begins at this level and soon progresses to more challenging work. Encourage the child to answer in sentences.
Answers:
1. The tailor was sitting at his window working.
2. An old woman came down the road.
3. She was selling honey.
4. It was morning.
5. Yes, he did like honey.
6. He put it on a slice of bread.
7. He put it on the table near him.

Missing letters (br) Answers:
bread, broom, brother, brush.
Ask the child to read out the words which s/he has made. Follow up by looking for things around the home and environment, which begin with 'br'.

Handwriting 2 - (*page 6*)
This does not look like handwriting! It provides practice in developing fluency and flow for joined script. The dotted lines should be traced, then the patterns copied in the spaces provided.

Feeling sheepish - (*page 7*) (Grammar)
Have fun with a well known rhyme! The speech bubbles in the cartoon version of *Little Boy Blue* show what the characters might have said. The child should enter what is said on the lines provided. *Key Stage 2 Grammar* provides more practice in identifying speech and using speech marks.
Answers:
Boy Blue where are you?
Where is the boy who looks after the sheep?
He's under the haystack fast asleep.
You lazy good for nothing. I'll marmalise you!

'ed' and 'ing' - (*page 8*) (Spelling)
Here is an activity which shows how words are changed by adding these endings. Point out the different ways in which this is done. Some words remain the same, and just have the ending added. Others need slight changes first. Most words ending in 'e' lose this before 'ing' is added. Some words have the last letter doubled.
Answers:
1. played playing
   cracked cracking
   looked looking
   fished fishing
   kicked kicking
   cooked cooking
   mended mending
2. shopped shopping
   tripped tripping
   hopped hopping
   clapped clapping
   chopped chopping
   chatted chatting
   rubbed rubbing
3. liked liking
   hoped hoping
   loved loving
   saved saving
   blamed blaming
   dined dining
   smiled smiling

Mischief zoo - (*page 9*) (Grammar)
Adjectives are describing words. The child is asked here to use the adjectives provided to describe the animals, in sentences which will make him/her laugh! Further practice with parts of speech, such as adjectives, appears in *Key Stage 2 Grammar*. Children who find this grammar work difficult, or the reading level too advanced could find more practice in *Key Stage 1 Creative Writing*.
Answers:
Do not walk across the striped zebra.
Do not teach the talking parrot rude words.
Wriggly snakes should not be used as scarves.
The flying bats should not be used for cricket.
This cage is reserved for naughty children.
Heads put in the ferocious lion's mouth cannot be replaced.

Handwriting 3 - (*page 10*)
Here attention is drawn to the differences in some letters when used for joined script, in particular 'f', 'y' and 'k'. The child should trace over the dotted lines, then copy the letters on the lines provided. More practice appears in *Key Stage 2 Handwriting*.

Crossword puzzle - (*page 11*)
Make sure that the child understands the 'rules' of crosswords: e.g. one letter per space, and that there are no clues for 1 down, 2 across, etc. because no words reading in these directions begin on these numbers. The numbers in brackets after the clues show the number of letters in the words. (Simpler crosswords appear in *Key Stage 1 Spelling*). Children who find crosswords easy could try some of the easier newspaper and magazine crosswords.
Answers:

© Folens.

The Lion and the Mouse - (*pages 12-13*) (Reading)
Read the story with the child. Encourage him/her to answer in sentences. *Key Stage 2 Reading* provides more practice at this level, and progresses to more challenging activities. If the child finds this difficult, *Key Stage 1 Reading* may provide activities in which s/he can succeed.
Answers:
1. The lion was asleep under a tree.
2. A (little) mouse ran over the lion's paw.
3. The lion was going to crush the mouse.
4. She said, "Please, please, do not kill me."
5. No, the lion did not believe her.
6. He walked into a trap.
7. He roared and roared when he could not free himself.
8. She nibbled through the ropes.
9. He thanked her and said, "You have saved my life."
10. Yes, they became great friends.

Blends - (*page 14*) (Spelling)
Blends of consonants are where 2 or more consonants go together, e.g. **gr**ass, **str**ing, **str**aw. This page shows blends of three consonants. It is useful if the child understands the difference between vowels and consonants before trying this activity. See *Key Stages 1 and 2 Spelling*.

You could help to develop his/her spelling of words with consonants by looking for them in everyday situations, perhaps playing 'I spy' games, where the initial 2 or 3 letters of everything 'spied' have to be consonant blends. In the activity on this page, it may help if the child crosses out each word as it is entered in its place on the chart. This avoids missing any.
Answers:

1. | **spl** | **scr** | **spr** | **str** |
    |---|---|---|---|
    | **spl**ash | **scr**ap | **spr**ing | **str**eam |
    | **spl**endid | **scr**ub | **spr**out | **str**ap |
    | **spl**inter | **scr**ew | **spr**ead | **str**ing |
    | | **scr**ape | **spr**ay | **str**ong |
2. **spl**int | **scr**atch | **spr**int | **str**eet

The case of the missing letters - (*page 15*) (Grammar)
Apostrophes replace missing letters. This provides examples where two words combine to make one, with some letters missed out.
Answers:
don't – do not
doesn't – does not
I'll – I will (or I shall)
what's – what is
I'm – I am
she's – she is
can't – cannot.

Passport - (*page 16*) (Writing)
We write in a range of styles for different purposes. This activity is one where full sentences are not required, just words and numbers. If possible show the child a real passport, noting how the writing used for the signature differs from the rest.

Spell 'ea' words - (*page 17*) (Spelling)
This is a useful development from the 'ee' words (page 3). Here the child should read all the words in one section, then cover them before filling in the gaps, using the pictures as a prompt in section 1. You could use the words from sections 2 and 3 as the basis for a spelling 'test'. Most of *Key Stage 2 Spelling* is at this level, with some more challenging activities introduced towards the end.

Action words - (*page 18*) (Grammar)
Action words describe things which are **done** (actions!). Here the child has to read each sentence looking for the actions, which s/he should underline.
Answers A:
1. chased
2. bought
3. (is) coming
4. went
5. (was) shining
6. fell, broke
7. jumped
8. sang.

Answers B: (possible answers)
1. cried, slept
2. caught, locked up, saw, chased
3. chased, caught, attacked
4. is growing, grows
5. wrote, read
6. gave
7. is, lives
8. won, lost, drew.

For more practice see *Key Stage 2 Grammar*.

Handwriting 4 - (*page 19*)
Here is more practice in letters for joined script. Note where the child should begin each letter, and the direction in which the pen or pencil should move.

Number plates - (*page 20*) (Spelling)
Spelling practice can be fun! Use this as a game when travelling. Take turns to make up words from number plates. Rule: keep the letters in the same order! Examples from those provided: **art**w**ork**, **carp**a**rk**, **stat**i**on**, **ston**e, **pers**o**n**, **dan**g**le**, **down**f**all**, **post**e**r**, **oper**a**tor**, **beau**t**iful**, **boas**t**ful**.

Asking questions - (*page 21*) (Grammar)
Understanding of punctuation is developed at a football match! The child has to decide which sentences are questions.
Answers:
Questions:
Did you see that foul?
Is it nearly half time?
Who wants a programme?
Is the referee stupid?

© Folens.

Where can I buy a pie?
The other sentences need full stops.

Handwriting 5 - (*page 22*)
Here is some more practice in joined script, where two letters are joined. See also *Key Stage 2 Handwriting*. Further practice in unjoined script appears mainly in *Key Stage 1 Handwriting*.

Wordsearch - (*page 23*) (Spelling)
Begin by reading the word list with the child, then ask him/her to write each word without looking at them.
Answers:
2.

a	c	a	r	e	o	w	i	t	h	e
r	p	w	w	e	n	t	i	n	c	e
c	g	i	v	e	w	a	n	t		i
w	l	i	t	l	e	a	f	t	e	r
g	h	a	v	e	a	w	a	h	t	n
m	t	o	n	w	l	i	t	t	l	e
s	h	s	a	i	d	w	g	i	v	w
a	w	e	c	o	m	e	g	n	a	r
a	w	v	e	r	y	o	w	a	s	r

3. 'w' words: went, with, was, want.
   3 lettered words: was, are.
   5 lettered word: after.

More practice at this level appears in *Key Stage 2 Spelling*.

Antonyms – opposites - (*page 24*)
Antonym means opposite in meaning. Note the suggestion that the child crosses off each word as it is used. This prevents any being missed or used twice.
Answers:

up	down	light	dark
back	front	old	new
top	bottom	hot	cold
fast	slow	under	over
high	low	left	right
fat	thin	before	after

Have fun with the child, talking in 'opposite speak', where words are replaced by their opposites, e.g. Go downstairs to bed. Switch on the dark.

On holiday - (*page 25*) (Writing)
Here the writing will require very short sentences, and could even be in note form, e.g. (Items to be taken) suntan oil - to stop sunburn. The child is required to consider the context and use skills of reasoning in deciding which items to pack and which to leave behind. Discussion of many everyday activities in addition to packing for different types of holiday, e.g. skiing, walking, could be used to develop these skills.

The swallows - (*page 26*) (Reading)
The child reads the passage and answers the questions. Some less demanding examples appear in *Key Stage 1*, and at the beginning of *Key Stage 2 Reading*, which progresses to this level and beyond. Encourage the child to answer in sentences.
Answers:
1. Swallows eat flies.
2. They can eat berries and seeds.
3. The blackbird feeds on rowan berries.
4. The robin likes rosehips.
5. The old barn was at the back of the farmer's house.
6. They built them in May.
7. It has strong wings to move through the sky like lightning.
8. They will return in the spring.

When? - (*page 27*) (Grammar)
This develops understanding of tenses: past, present and future, and how the spellings of the verbs (action words) change. For more practice see *Key Stage 2 Writing*. Note that although the people are from the past, they could have been speaking in any tense.
Answers:
Past:
King Alfred, Sir Walter Raleigh.
Future:
Hannibal, Cleopatra.
Present:
Florence Nightingale, Martin Luther King.

How go you get there? - (*page 28*) (Grammar)
Here the purpose of writing is to give clear, simple instructions which could be followed by another person. Further activities providing examples of writing for a range of purposes appear in *Key Stage 2 Grammar*. Try giving the child directions when you are going somewhere new, and see if s/he can follow them, telling you where to turn and when to go straight on. Ask him/her to write instructions for getting to places in the neighbourhood, then to try them out with you, to see how accurate they were.
Answers:
'Start at F'. The destination is D (grocer).
There are several ways to get from the Post Office (A) to the butcher's (G): e.g. Walk **south** along Lords Lane. Turn **east** at Queens Avenue. Walk along Queens Avenue. Turn **south** at Royal Row. Walk along Royal Row. Stop at the shop after Kings Road.

© Folens.